EVEN MORE LITTLE PEPPERS

Elissa Milne

This book is dedicated to Georgina Zellan-Smith, who developed precision in my musical thinking without stifling my original voice.

© 2004 by Faber Music Ltd
First published in 2004 by Faber Music Ltd
3 Queen Square London WC1N 3AU
Music processed by MusicSet 2000
Cover illustration by Dave Wood
Printed in England by Caligraving Ltd

0-571-52315-3

To buy Faber Music publications or to find out about the full range of titles available
please contact your local music retailer or Faber Music sales enquiries:

Faber Music Limited, Burnt Mill, Elizabeth Way, Harlow, CM20 2HX England
Tel: +44 (0)1279 82 89 82   Fax: +44 (0)1279 82 89 83
sales@fabermusic.com   fabermusic.com

FABER _ff_ MUSIC

NO WORRIES

Elissa Milne

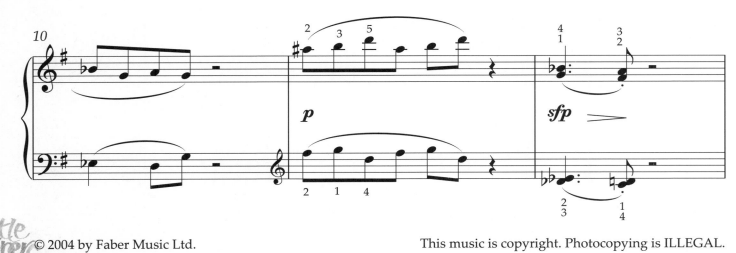

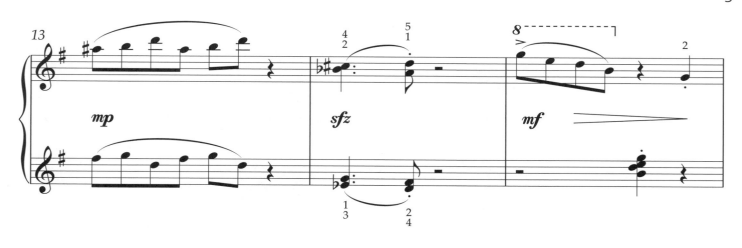

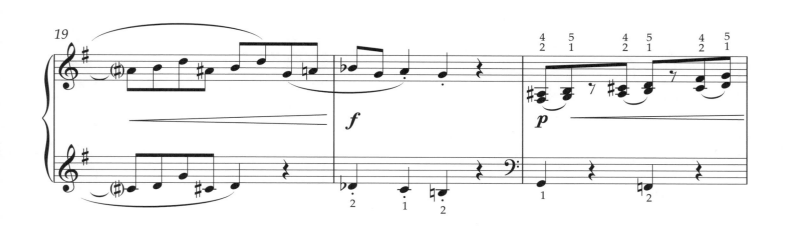

ZIGZAG

LIZARD

JUNGLE JINGLE

BUMBLEBLUE

molto rit.

ASHES

Rhumba ♩=112 ✓

LARRIKIN

A larrikin is someone who is a little mischievious and might get up to a prank or two!

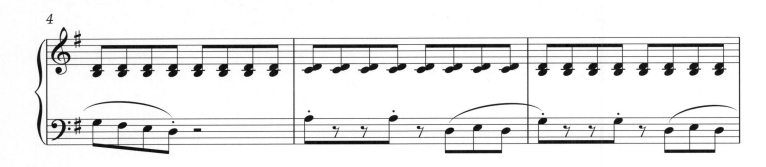

ADRIFT

HAVE A NICE DAY

CHATTERBOX

Garrulously ♩ = *c*.112

PEAS IN A POD *

* See page 24 for a note on how to play this piece. This page may be photocopied to avoid page-turns.

23

INDEX

TO THE TEACHER

Elissa Milne's *Little Peppers* series is a graded sequence of exciting performance pieces designed to introduce beginner pianists to essential technical skills. For more details and a CD of complete performances, see the *Guided tour of the Little Peppers*: ISBN 0-571-52332-3.

NOTE ON PLAYING *PEAS IN A POD*

Peas in a pod has been composed in eight equal parts so you can enjoy arranging the music yourself. You can play these parts in any order, miss out a part or play each more than once (though bear in mind that parts I, II, III, V, VI and VIII sound best to finish with). This means that your version of *Peas in a pod* might be much shorter than in this book, or even much longer!

What's more, because all the parts work well with each other, you can play this piece as a duet (two players on one piano), a duo (two players on two pianos), or even with three or four people playing simultaneously! Each player should start on a different part; experiment until you find your favourite combination. Alternatively, you may want to try playing the piece straight through as written; in which case, it will work simultaneously with the *Peas in a pod* from any of the other *Little Peppers* books! Whatever you decide, have fun with creating your own *Peas in a pod*.